Animals coloring book for kids

This book belongs to

Thank you.

We hope you enjoyed our book.

As a small family company, your feedback is
very important to us.

Please let us know how you like our book at:
adrian.stoica@deannaosc.com

www.ingramcontent.com/pod-product-compliance
Lightning Source LLC
Chambersburg PA
CBHW081629250726
48657CB00009B/2788